The Voice of God's Creation

Betty J. Hurst

Kingdom Builders Publications LLC

This Book Belongs to

Dedication

I dedicate this book to my husband, Bobby Hurst, who is my great supporter, to the family of the late Hattie Fruster, who encouraged me to follow my dreams, and to my younger brother Squeeky, whom I love dearly.

Day One (Uno)
1
Night and Day

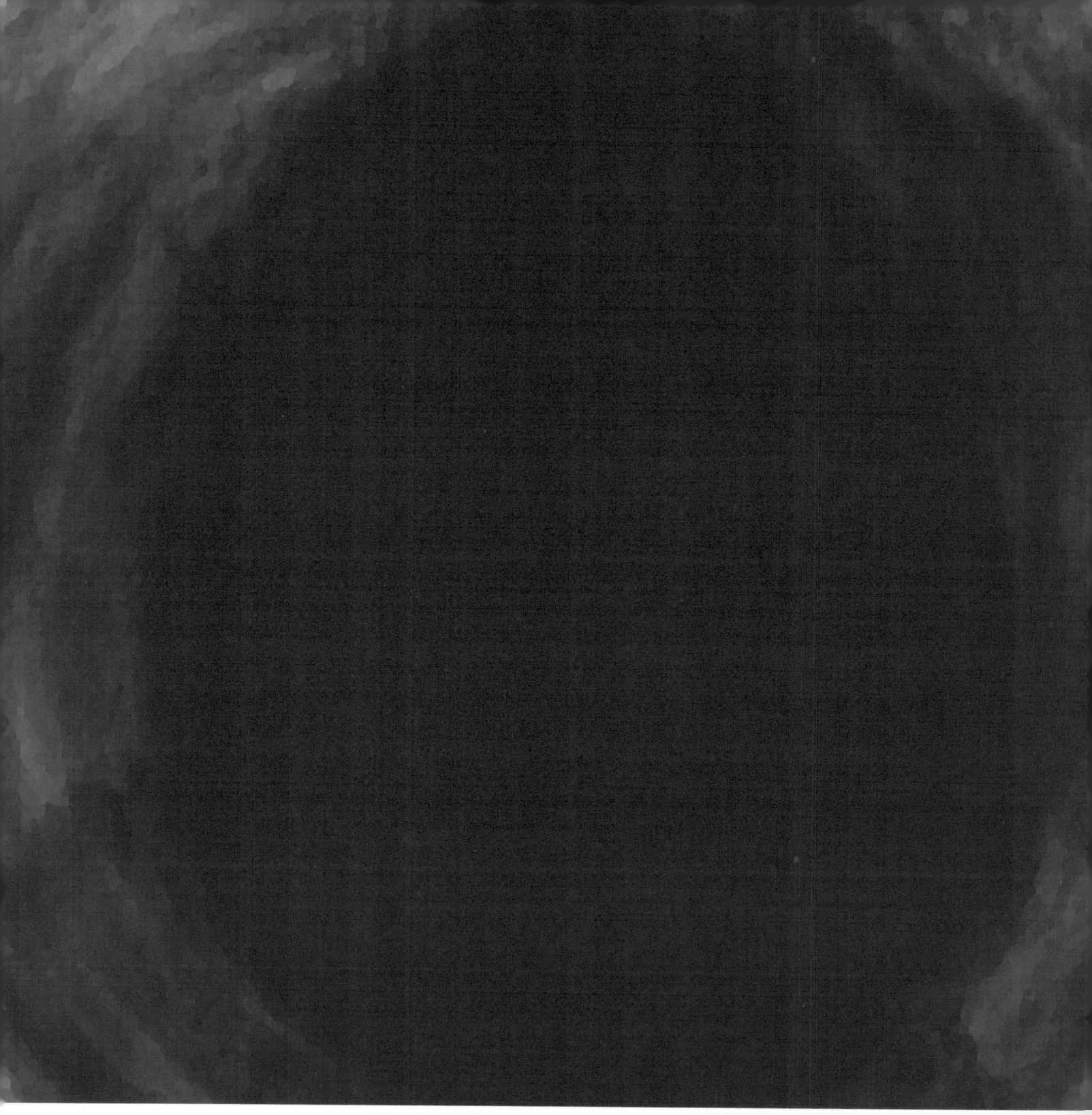

In the beginning, God made the
Heavens and the Earth in seven days.

Greater light - Day

Lesser light - Night

The world was colorless! When "less" is at the end of a word, it means without. Without color means it was pitch darkness. And the Voice of God said, "Light appear!"

midday / noon

12 midday 12:00

pm

morning

afternoon

DAY

sunrise

sunset

dawn

6 am
06:00

6 pm
18:00

dusk

NIGHT

morning

evening

am

12 midnight 00:00

midnight

Periods of the Day
Morning
Dawn
Sunrise
Noon
Sunset
Dusk
Midnight
Twilight

And the Voice of God said, "This is good."

Day Two (Dos)

2

The Sky and the Sea

Look at the firmament. A firmament is where Heaven (sky) meets the ground. The sky and the waters are holding hands. You can see this when you go to a beach, ocean, or sea.

Sky from Water

Mist

Fog

Clouds

Rain

Water from Waters

Stream

Lake

River

Sea

Ocean

RIVER

OCEAN

STREAM

SEA

And the Voice of God said, "Let us divide the waters."

God organized the water from the waters.

And the Voice of God said, "This is good."

Day Three (Tres)
3
Land and Vegetation

And the Voice of God said, "Grass, herbs, trees, and plants come forth."

Day Four (Cuatro)

4

The Stars, the Sun, and the Moon

The Voice of God named the Seasons.

Spring   Summer   Autumn (Fall)   Winter

The Voice of God named the Days.

Sunday Monday Tuesday Wednesday
Thursday Friday Saturday

1 day = 24 hours
1 week = 7 days
1 month = 30 days
12 months = 1 year
1 year = 365 days

Day Five (Cinco)
5
Sea Creatures and Birds

The Voice of God created moving creatures.
He created the fish in the sea and the fowls
in the air.
And the Voice of God blessed them. He said,
"Be blessed and multiply in the sea and in
the sky."

Day Six (Seis)

6

Animals and Humans

And the Voice of God made animals of all kind.

The Voice of God said, "This is good."

The Day of Man

The Voice of God said, "Let's make mankind in our image and likeness."

Then they may name and rule over the fish in the sea and the birds in the sky, over the livestock and all the wild animals, and over all the creatures that move along the ground.

God blessed them and said to them, "Be fruitful and increase in number; fill the earth and subdue (control) it. Rule over the fish in the sea and the birds in the sky and over every living creature that moves on the ground."

Then God said, "I give you every seed-bearing plant on the face of the whole earth and every tree that has fruit with seed in it. They will be yours for food.

And to all the beasts of the earth and all the birds in the sky and all the creatures that move along the ground—everything that has the breath of life in it—I give every green plant for food."

The Voice of God created the ground for animals to walk on and the sea for animals to swim in.

1st — He made the water.
2nd — He made the ground for vegetation.
3rd — He made the creeping animals.
4th — He made us from the ground.

Herds of cow, sheep, and horses

Fish

Hamster

Frog

Lizard

Seagull

Butterfly

Man was given 3 jobs:

❖ To be fruitful and multiply. This means to make many.

❖ To name the vegetation and animals.

❖ To take care of the land.

Day Seven (Siete)

7

Rest

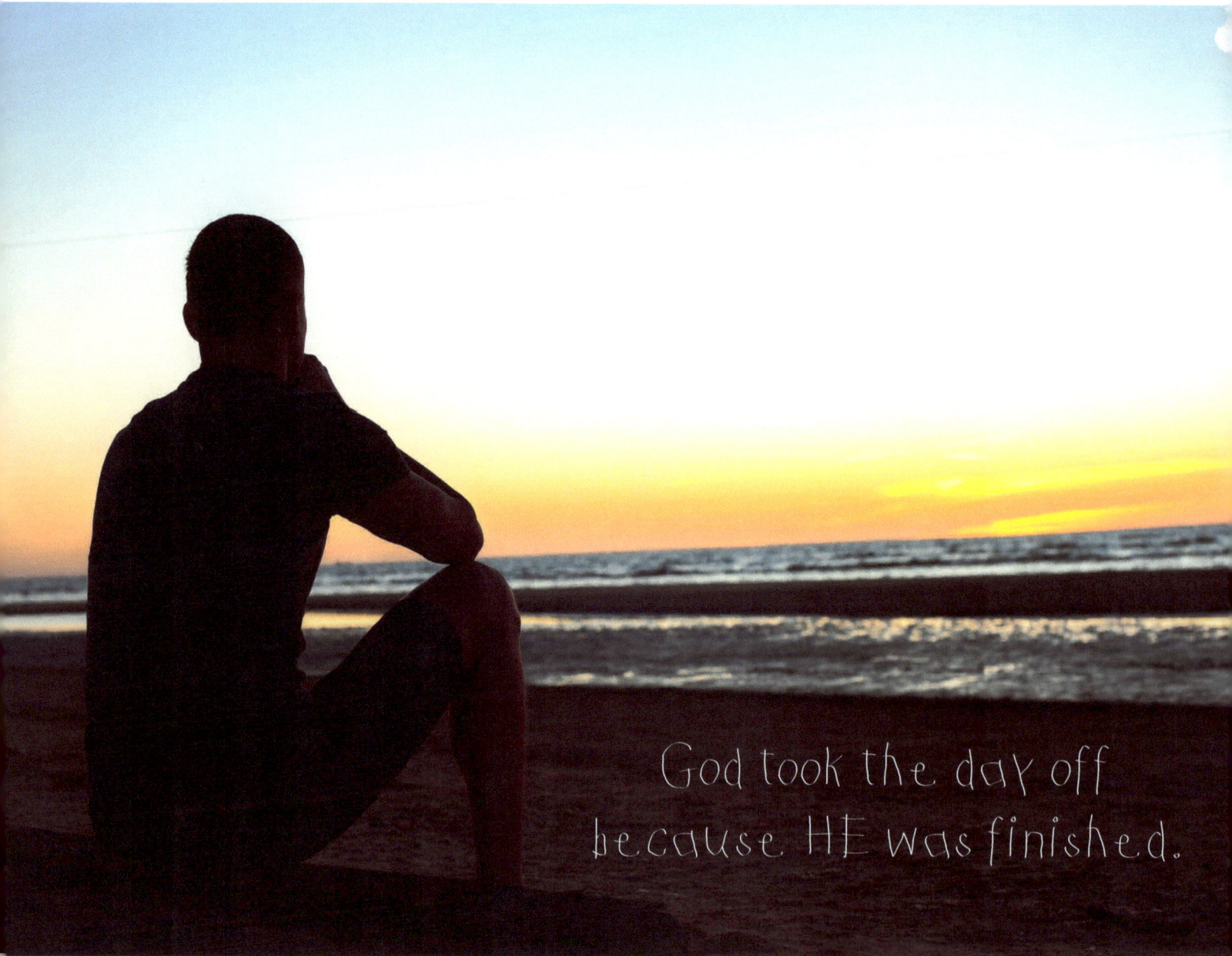

God took the day off
because HE was finished.

God made the Heavens and the Earth in seven days.

ABOUT THE AUTHOR

Betty Jenkins Hurst was born in Holly Hill, SC to Pinkie and Lody.

When Betty was twelve, she moved to Miami, Florida to be with her sisters after the death of their mother. She completed high school and went on to graduate from the Robert Fiance Beauty School in 1987. In 1989, she got her CDL license to drive a school bus. She carried elementary through high school special needs students to school each day. She considered them as her precious cargo. Betty retired in 2016 from Richland School District 2 with over 30 years of service.

Betty met her husband of 34 years in Miami. They have one son and three grandsons. She is a minister in her local assembly. She has a great compassion for the homeless and is an excellent caregiver.

Betty loves reading, writing, watching basketball, cooking, and studying the Bible.

www.ingramcontent.com/pod-product-compliance
Lightning Source LLC
Chambersburg PA
CBHW042010090426
42811CB00015B/1604